T0104284

Ant
Antics

FIRST EDITION
Series Editor Deborah Lock; **US Editor** Shannon Beatty; **Designer** Jemma Westing;
Production Editor Sean Daly; **Picture Researcher** Rob Nunn; **Jacket Designer** Natalie Godwin;
Natural History Consultant Tom Fayle; **Reading Consultant** Linda Gambrell, PhD

THIS EDITION
Editorial Management by Oriel Square
Produced for DK by WonderLab Group LLC
Jennifer Emmett, Erica Green, Kate Hale, *Founders*

Editors Grace Hill Smith, Libby Romero, Michaela Weglinski;
Photography Editors Kelley Miller, Annette Kiesow, Nicole DiMella; **Managing Editor** Rachel Houghton;
Designers Project Design Company; **Researcher** Michelle Harris; **Copy Editor** Lori Merritt;
Indexer Connie Binder; **Proofreader** Larry Shea; **Reading Specialist** Dr. Jennifer Albro;
Curriculum Specialist Elaine Larson

Published in the United States by DK Publishing
1745 Broadway, 20th Floor, New York, NY 10019
Copyright © 2023 Dorling Kindersley Limited
DK, a Division of Penguin Random House LLC
22 23 24 25 26 10 9 8 7 6 5 4 3 2 1
001–333465–May/2023

A catalog record for this book
is available from the Library of Congress.
HC ISBN: 978-0-7440-6829-0
PB ISBN: 978-0-7440-6830-6

DK books are available at special discounts when purchased in bulk for sales promotions, premiums,
fundraising, or educational use. For details, contact: DK Publishing Special Markets,
1745 Broadway, 20th Floor, New York, NY 10019
SpecialSales@dk.com

Printed and bound in China

The publisher would like to thank the following for their kind permission to reproduce their images:
a=above; c=center; b=below; l=left; r=right; t=top; b/g=background

Shutterstock.com: Fourleaflover 6–7b

Cover image: *Front:* **Dreamstime.com:** ActiveLines; **Shutterstock.com:** frank60 r, Peter F Wolf bl;
Back: **Dreamstime.com:** Tomacco cra, cl

All other images © Dorling Kindersley
For more information see: www.dkimages.com

For the curious
www.dk.com

Ant Antics

Deborah Lock

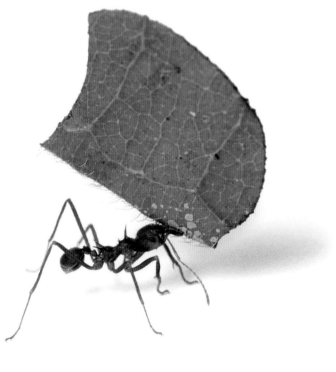

Contents

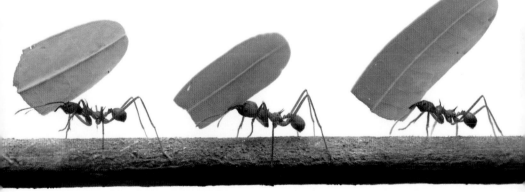

Ants Alive!

Ants have been on Earth for more than 110 million years. They've spread out all over the planet, and there's about 10,000 trillion of them crawling around.

Red Fire Ants
We thrive all over the world. Meet us on page 22.

Carpenter Ants
We are found all over the world. Meet us on page 28.

Leafcutter Ants
We live in Central and South America. Meet us on page 16.

More than 12,000 different kinds of ants have been named and there are probably many thousands more. They survive by working together in colonies. Each tiny ant has a job to keep the whole colony going. Find out about the amazing busy lives of six different ants.

Army Ants
We live in tropical regions. Meet us on page 8.

Weaver Ants
We live in Africa, Asia, and Australia. Meet us on page 34.

Bulldog Ants
Our colonies are mostly found in Australia. Meet us on page 40.

Swarm Raiders

Get out of our way or else!

We're army ants, and we're always on the hunt for food. If you were a small animal in our path, you'd have no chance, even if you were bigger than us.

First, we'd overwhelm you with our numbers. There are more than 200,000 of us on a raid. Then, we'd cut and slice you into tiny pieces. That way, we can carry the pieces back to our nest.

Ant Senses

Ants have poor eyesight but amazing antennae that feel around and pick up smells. Ants use their antennae to find their prey, know where they are, and communicate with each other.

We might be tiny, but it takes us less than 10 minutes to cut up a 2-inch (5-cm) long spider and take it away to our nest. We leave nothing where the attack took place. We know our way back to the nest. We follow the scent trail we left as we fanned out across the forest floor.

Large soldier ants line our trail
and are ready to protect us if we are
attacked. They have much larger
mandibles than us—the worker ants.

mandible

Back at the nest, we hand over the pieces to the smaller workers. They crush the pieces and squeeze out the liquids. They feed the liquids to our queen and the rest of the colony.

Living Nests

Army ants make living nests. By linking together, they form walls and tunnels. This keeps their queen and her 120,000 eggs and young protected.

Our nest is unusual. Look closely, and you'll notice it's made up of thousands of ants. When we rest, we fasten onto each other, using the hooks and spines on our mandibles and on our feet.

There could be more than 1 million ants in one colony.

The site of our nest is only temporary. Once we've raided an area and can find no more food, we all move on. We mostly march at night in a long column, protected by the soldiers. We're just like an army.

Some workers carry the queen and her eggs. Others carry the larvae.

Some workers go on ahead to check out the area. They leave a scent trail for the rest of us to follow. In the daylight, we set up camp again, linking together to make a new nest.

Now we're ready to go out raiding again.

Quick! March!

Fungus Farmers

Make way! We're coming through with our heavy load. These pieces of leaves might not look heavy to you, but they're five times our body weight.

We're leafcutter ants, and we're all very busy. We carry the leaves to our nest. Smaller workers sit on top to stop flies from landing on the leaves.
It takes us several hours to scuttle back and forth from our nest to where the large workers are slicing off the pieces.

These workers cut the leaves with razor-sharp teeth on their mandibles, which powerfully vibrate a thousand times per second.

A Heavy Load
Leafcutter ants can carry pieces at least 10 times their body weight, which is the same as a human carrying a small car.

Once at the nest, we take our pieces underground and hand them over to some other workers. We don't eat the leaves. We use them as compost to grow a certain type of fungus. The fungus is our food.

The underground workers grow
the fungus. To do this, they cut and chew
the leaves into a gooey pulp. They take
great care to spread out the leaf pulp.
They cover it with our droppings, and then
place a small piece of fungus on top.

Fussy Fungus
Different types of leafcutter
ants grow different types of
fungus. If the fungus does
not like a leaf, it produces
a chemical that the ants
sense. Then, the ants find
other leaves to collect.

There are millions of us in the colony and we're all sisters. Our mother, the queen ant, lays thousands of eggs every day. The younger workers look after them.

Our nest covers a large area and has several entrances. Inside, we've dug out hundreds of chambers that are about the size of a soccer ball. We grow the fungus inside these chambers.

Our large soldiers protect us from enemies, such as hunter spiders and other ants, by biting them hard.

The small, young workers are the nurses, moving and cleaning the eggs and feeding the larvae.

We create huge amounts of waste because there are so many of us. Some workers remove all the old fungus and waste. They either bury it deep within the nest or pile it up outside. Workers move it around so that it breaks down into soil quickly.

The rest of us don't go near these workers. We don't want to catch the germs and diseases that may infect the leaves and fungus.

More leaves are needed now.

Off we go again!

Fiery Team Workers

I wouldn't step on our nest if I were you. You don't want to upset us because we can get very angry. And when we're angry, we each use our weapon—a poisoned stinger! We are red fire ants, and we are found all over the world.

When we attack, we grasp our victim with our mandibles. Then, we inject venom from our stinger. We turn on our heads and sting around in a circle. Our poison can kill small creatures. It can cause a burning pain in humans, too.

Our colony was started by a young queen and a group of worker ants in just one day.

Our queen has been laying 1,500 eggs a day, which hatch into larvae.

The larvae later become adults. Then, these young workers start looking after the queen, the eggs, and the larvae. They keep the colony clean, too.

Our colony grows quickly. After three years, there are 60,000 of us.

You might think we are troublemakers because we infest farmland and hurt you. However, we are successful because we are organized and work together as a team.

Older workers have the most dangerous job. We go out and search for food. We eat everything—animals and plants—squeezing out the liquids to suck. Working together, we can attack and kill a lizard in less than a minute.

Many of us stay inside the nest, digging out new chambers and tunnels to make room for our growing colony. Sometimes, our nests have more than one queen, so our colonies can have half a million ants. To make room, we dig deeper and deeper. Some of our nests can be 5-feet (1.5-m) deep.

We push the soil up to the surface, leaving mounds more than 3-feet (1-m) high above the ground. Quite an achievement for tiny creatures! So please, don't step on us. Be impressed and keep your distance.

A red fire ant's abdomen is darker than the rest of its body.

Wood Tunnelers

We don't eat wood. That's the truth! We just break it up to make tunnels and chambers for our nest.

As they nest and tunnel out the wood, a large colony of carpenter ants may be heard rustling or gnawing.

We are carpenter ants, and we make nests for our queen in moist wood. Her eggs need moisture so that they don't dry out. Most of us live outside in rotting trees, roots, and logs.

We do come indoors and can do terrible damage to your homes and other buildings. Also, as our colony grows, we make other nests for just the workers and larvae in other wooden boards or beams.

Nest Sites
Indoors, carpenter ant nests can be found in damp or hollow places, such as under roofs, in doors and walls, and around sinks, showers, and dishwashers.

apple core

We're attracted into your homes
by the sweet-tasting foods you have.
Honey, jelly, and sugar are our
favorites. Outside, we find little
insects called aphids, which ooze
sweet honeydew when we stroke
them. We also feed on other insects,
cutting them into small pieces and
squeezing them for the juices.

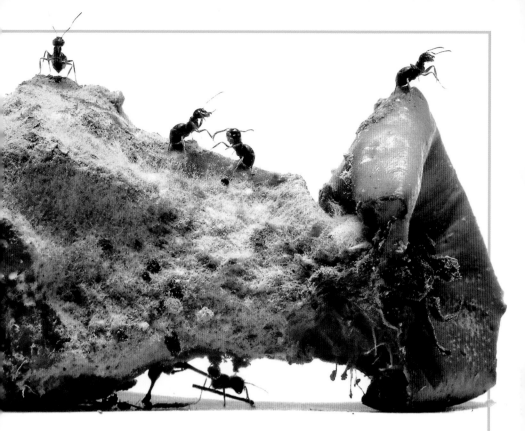

Like all ants, we have two stomachs: one for our own food supply and another for food to bring back up and share with the colony. We're most active during the spring and summer, going out at night to look for food to bring back to the nest.

In late summer, workers try to collect more food so that many of the larvae can be well fed. These well-fed larvae develop into winged queen and male ants.

The following spring, when the weather is warm and humid after rain, the winged ants fly from the nest. They travel far and wide. Winged ants from other nests do this at the same time.

In great swarms, the queens mate with the male ants. Afterward, the male ants die and the queens find suitable damp homes for their new colonies. I'll bet you're hoping this will not be indoors!

Weaving Wonders

Hold on! Pull! Nearly there! Pull!

    We're weaver ants, and the most amazing thing about us is how we make our treetop nests.

    Have you ever tried sewing together a bag? Well, you take a piece of material—in our case, that's a leaf—and then fold it over, so that the edges can be sewn together. There needs to be many, many workers for us to do this.

We line up along an edge of a leaf and hold it very tightly in our mandibles. Then, we begin to bend the leaf edge over toward the other edge. More workers join us, linking to our feet and helping us to pull until the edges are nearly touching.

Then, yet more workers bring larvae from our old nest and gently squeeze them. A thin thread of silk oozes out from each larva. We then work on sticking the edges of the leaf together, using the silk.

Our nests can be very large, as we then begin connecting another leaf and then another. Sometimes, our nests connect branches from two trees. **Impressed?**

We don't damage the tree. In fact, we protect it. We stop other animals from coming to live in the tree or eating parts of it.

Tasty Snack
Some people eat the eggs and pupae of the weaver ants. The eggs and pupae taste like lemon—juicy and a little bit sour.

We have many enemies that try to trick us, though. Some caterpillars produce a sweet liquid called honeydew, which we love to eat. While we are distracted eating the honeydew, they crawl into the nest to eat our larvae.

Jumping spiders smell like us, so they are able to enter our nest undetected to eat the eggs, larvae, and us. It's tough being an ant!

Jumping spiders don't make webs but stealthily hunt for their food.

Speedy Hunters

We can see you!

Unlike other kinds of ants, we have large eyes and excellent eyesight. We are bulldog ants, and we are one of the largest kinds. We are as aggressive as wasps. In fact, scientists believe ants are close relatives of bees and wasps. Although we don't have wings, we hunt and sting and live in nests just like them.

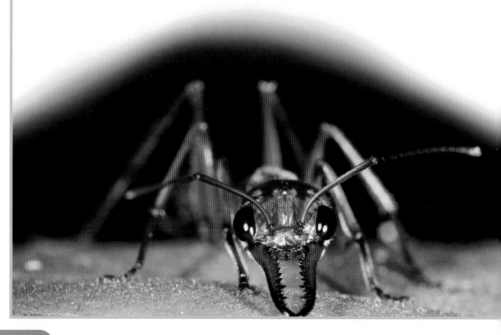

We hunt on our own, tracking
other insects like a spy. When the
moment is right, quick-as-a-flash,
we scuttle forward to bite our victim
and bend our backs to inflict our
sting. Our stings are very powerful,
and the venom acts quickly to
paralyze our prey.

We carry our victim back to our nest. Our prey can be seven times as heavy as us. The insect is chewed up and fed to the larvae. They are the meat eaters.

Our colony only has about 1,000 ants, so we all work hard to find enough food. When the colony is small, even our queen takes care of the eggs and her larvae and goes out of the nest to hunt.

We all protect our nest from attacks. When we are annoyed, we leap around. We also chase after spiders and cockroaches to scare them off and get them away from our nest.

Other ants are our fiercest enemies. Although they are much smaller than we are, they can overwhelm us with their great numbers. But we don't give up easily. Even if our bodies are split in half, our heads continue to bite and our tails lash out to sting.

Like all ants, we fight for the survival of our colony, fearlessly facing death.

Glossary

Antennae
Moveable parts on an insect's head that pick up senses

Bivouac
[bi-VOO-ak]
An army ants' nest created by linking together their own bodies [The term also means an army camp that is set up for a short time]

Colony
A group of ants that live together

Compost
A pile of rotting plants and animals that becomes fine soil that is full of nutrients

Fungus
A plant-like living thing, such as a toadstool or mold, that does not make its own food but lives on decaying plants and animals

Honeydew
A sweet, sticky liquid that oozes out of aphids and other small scaly insects

Larva
The newly hatched legless form of an ant

Mandibles
The mouthparts of an insect used for grabbing, biting, cutting, and chewing food

Paralyze
To make an animal unable to move

Prey
An animal hunted or captured for food

Queen ant
A female ant that lays the eggs

Raid
A surprise, sudden attack by an army

Regurgitate
To bring food that has been swallowed back up again into the mouth

Soldier ant
The largest ants of the colony that protect the worker ants and defend the nest from intruders

Stinger
A sharp-pointed tip of an ant's abdomen that can prick a victim and inject venom

Swarm
A large number of flying insects

Tropical
An area where the climate is hot and humid all year around

Venom
A poisonous liquid that some ants inject into their victim by stinging

Worker ant
The smaller ants of the colony that look after the queen, the eggs, and larvae; dig out the chambers of the nest; and forage for food

Index

Quiz

Answer the questions to see what you have learned. Check your answers in the key below.

1. How do army ants know the way back to their nest?

2. True or False: Leafcutter ants eat the leaves they collect.

3. What do leafcutter ants grow in their colonies?

4. What is a red fire ant's lethal weapon?

5. Where do carpenter ants make nests for their queen?

6. When are carpenter ants most active?

7. Name two enemies that try to trick weaver ants.

8. Which ant has large eyes and excellent eyesight?

1. They follow a scent trail 2. False 3. Fungus
4. A poisoned stinger 5. In moist wood 6. Spring and summer
7. Caterpillars and jumping spiders 8. Bulldog ants